CONTENTS

Any words appearing in the text in bold, **like this**, are explained in the Glossary. You can also look out for them in the Word Bank at the bottom of each page.

LARGE SCALE

Organized crime covers all sorts of activities. From street gangs to large criminal organizations working across the world, they all use bullying and fear to get their way. They deal in:

- car theft
- robbery
- drug dealing
- **smuggling** weapons, people or works of art
- gambling
- **fraud**, blackmail and bank crimes.

The bald man with a scar down his face looks up. He calmly strokes the white cat on his lap. His voice is soft. 'Allow me to introduce myself. I am Ernst Blofeld. They told me you were killed in Hong Kong. You only live twice, Mr Bond.'

The scene is from the James Bond film *You Only Live Twice*. Ernst Blofeld is the boss of Spectre, an organization whose members know each other only by code numbers. All the members are wanted by the police for their crimes in many countries around the world. Any who do not show trust in Blofeld are swiftly **executed**.

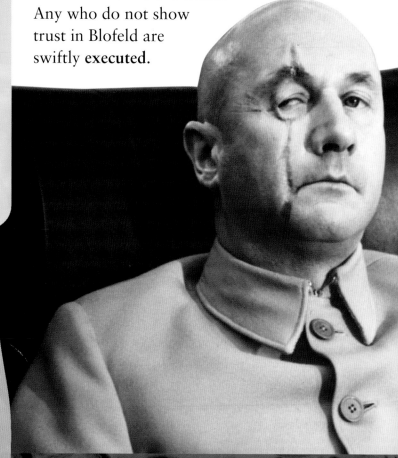

WORD BANK

executed   killed as a punishment
fiction   made-up story from the imagination

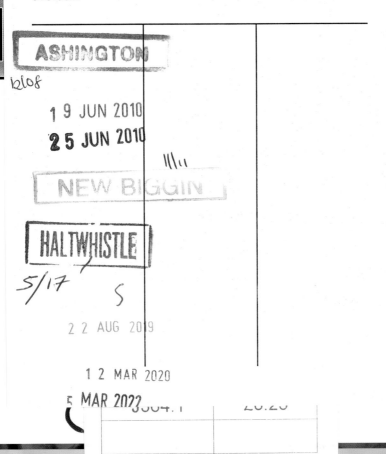
John Townsend

www.raintreepublishers.co.uk
Visit our website to find out more information about **Raintree** books.

To order:
 Phone 44 (0) 1865 888113
 Send a fax to 44 (0) 1865 314091
 Visit the Raintree Bookshop at **www.raintreepublishers.co.uk** to browse our catalogue and order online.

First published in Great Britain by
Raintree, Halley Court, Jordan Hill, Oxford OX2 8EJ,
part of Harcourt Education.
Raintree is a registered trademark of Harcourt
Education Ltd.

© Harcourt Education Ltd 2004
First published in paperback in 2005.
The moral right of the proprietor has been asserted.

Editorial: Melanie Copland and Kate Buckingham
Design: Michelle Lisseter and Kamae Design
Picture Research: Maria Joannou and
Ginny Stroud-Lewis
Index: Indexing Specialists (UK) Ltd
Production: Jonathan Smith

Originated by Dot Gradations
Printed and bound in China
by South China Printing Company

ISBN 1 844 43591 1 (hardback)
08 07 06 05 04
10 9 8 7 6 5 4 3 2 1

ISBN 1 844 43597 0 (paperback)
09 08 07 06 05
10 9 8 7 6 5 4 3 2 1

British Library Cataloguing in Publication Data
Townsend, John
Organized Crime – (True Crime)
364.1'06
A full catalogue record for this book is available from
the British Library.

Acknowledgements
Alamy pp. **42** (Ron Chaple), **27** (Tobias Hohenacker);
Associated Press pp. **24–25**, **40**, **26** (Vincent Yu);
Corbis pp. **6–7** (Alain Schein Photography), **8–9**,
12–13, **40–41**, **4–5**, **5**, **11**, **19** (Bettmann), **22** (Diego
Lezama Orezzoni), **33** (George H H Huey), **30–31**
(Greg Smith), **15**, **28** (Harcourt Index), **10–11**, **16–17**
(Hulton Deutsch), **5**, **32** (Mona Reeder Dallas
Morning News), **33** (Nathan Benn), **41** (Niall
MacLeod), **6** (Peter Turnley), **35** (Reuters), **8**, **25**, **31**
(Ric Ergonbright), **18** (Richard T Nowitz), **36–37**
(Yves Forestier); Hulton Archive pp. **43** (American
Stock/Archive Photos), **20** (Harry Todd); Hutchinson
Library pp. **26–27** (Michael Macintyre); Interpol
p. **37**; Lonely Planet p. **24** (John Hay); PA Photos/EPA
pp. **30**, **19**, **34**; Peter Newark's American Pictures
pp. **10**, **12**, **13**; Photodisc/Harcourt Index p. **23**;
The Kobal Collection pp. **16**, **21**, **15**, **38**, **39**;
Tudor Photography p. **9**.

Cover photograph of dollar bills reproduced with
permission of Robert Harding Picture Library/
Digital Vision

Every effort has been made to contact copyright
holders of any material reproduced in this book.
Any omissions will be rectified in subsequent
printings if notice is given to the publishers.

The paper used to print this book comes from
sustainable resources.

THE REAL WORLD

In the film, Spectre deals in theft, kidnapping and **blackmail** to make money. But Spectre does not really exist. Ian Fleming, the writer of the James Bond stories, made up the name. It is just **fiction**. The bad news is that there are organizations around today just like Spectre. They may not be run by men with white cats, but they do have violent members who will kill anyone who gets in their way. These groups want money and power. They will do anything to get both. This is the world of big-time **organized crime**.

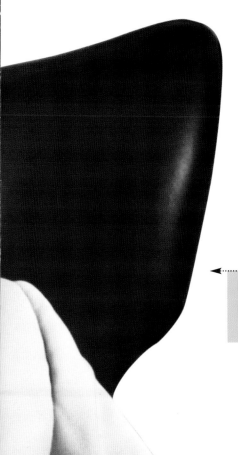

No one argues with Ernst Blofeld!

FIND OUT LATER...

Who were the gangsters of the past?

What are the mysteries of the Mafia?

What threats from organized crime face us today?

Organized crime involves people working together. It is run like a proper business. Each person has a set job, with an overall boss. These organizations are called gangs but they are nothing like noisy, unruly mobs. These gangs are **professional**.

A large garage, for example, might not be all it seems. It may sell top-of-the-range cars. But, it may also be dealing in stolen goods and drugs – from the criminal **underworld**.

The real problem comes when one gang upsets another. If there are **rival** gangs in the same city, the bullets start to fly. That is when anyone can get hurt, and they often do.

YOUTH GANGS

In the 20th century, street youth gangs grew in Los Angeles and other cities in the USA. The Bloods and the Crips are well-known youth gangs of Los Angeles. Many of them have bad reputations for being involved in organized crime.

The police are always on the tail of gang members.

WORD BANK   loyalty   never letting anyone down and always showing commitment

DOWN TOWN

Many of the gangs at work today are part of multi-million dollar organizations. They have taken years to grow into big businesses. But how did they all start?

Gangs of criminals joining up to make money are nothing new. The first cities had **bandit** gangs. Robbers worked together to protect each other. Many of them came from the poorer areas of town, where robbing and murder became a way of life. Joining a gang gave someone protection and a sense of belonging. It also gave them the chance to get rich from more daring crimes.

PASSING THE TEST

To join a gang like the Crips, people have to learn the rules and pass a test. This is called 'the knowledge'. They must swear **loyalty**. This may mean committing a crime or risking their lives. Then they perform a test of bravery. For example, the new **recruits** must walk along a line of gang members who take it in turns to beat and kick them. If they make it, they are in!

Stealing and selling cars is just one activity for organized criminals.

CHICAGO

Gangs of criminals were big trouble in some US cities. At the end of the 19th century, people flooded into the USA from across the world. Most **immigrants** were honest and hard-working but some were not. In the poorest areas, people turned to anger, greed and violence.

Chicago became one of the centres of organized street crime. Many Italians came to the city to start businesses. If they had a visit from The Black Hand (*La Mano Nera*), it was bad news. The Black Hand was a gang that demanded money. People had to pay up to protect themselves. If not, an armed mob would call round.

FROM BAD TO WORSE

Gangs got rich by running dishonest businesses. They demanded money and used threats. Their money-making schemes were called **racketeering**. This name was used after some New York gangs held dinners to make money. These became known as 'rackets' because of all the noise they made. Gambling, drinking and **bribing** the police, lawyers and politicians made matters worse.

All alcohol had to be poured away by law.

WORD BANK bootlegging smuggling illegal alcohol

GETTING A HOLD

At the start of 1915, The Black Hand gang set off 55 bombs in Chicago. They were trying to show who was boss. Some Italian Americans set up the **rival** White Hand gang to fight back. The streets became dangerous. Rowdy gangs attracted drunken mobs.

The US Government had to act. In 1920, it made a law banning the sale of alcohol. But this was just what the crime gangs needed. They began to make, sell and **smuggle** beer and whisky. There was a lot of money to be made from this. As a result, Chicago now had some of the most ruthless American **gangsters** in history.

THE 1920s

The time when alcohol was banned in the USA was called **prohibition**. It was against the law to make or sell alcoholic drinks like whisky, rum or beer. So that was just what criminals began to do. This was called **bootlegging** after the whisky smugglers of long ago who hid bottles in their long boots.

prohibition when something is forbidden – such as making and selling alcohol

AL CAPONE

One of the most famous men in 1920s Chicago was Al Capone. As a teenager, Capone was part of the dreaded Five Points Gang of New York. In 1919, he joined another gang that controlled the south of Chicago. He was just twenty. A few years later he was a big-time gangland boss in Chicago.

Capone's career of terror lasted through the 1920s. Money, power and murder made him public enemy number one. He made a fortune from smuggling alcohol. His **illegal** gambling bars were open day and night. He was soon making over $100,000 a week.

A CITY JUST RIGHT FOR CRIME

At the start of the 20th century, gangs in downtown Chicago (above) became so well-organized that the police could not deal with them properly. They could not cope with such a lot of crime. The police made many mistakes and the criminals were soon running the city.

The horrors of gang crime on Valentine's Day 1929.

WORD BANK

illegal   against the law
massacre   killing of lots of people

MURDER

No one got an important job in Chicago unless Capone said so. Some people thought he was a hero. Other gangs hated his power. One gang leader, 'Bugs' Moran, began to plot against him. Capone decided to act first.

On 14 February 1929, he sent his gang over. They dressed as policemen and gunned down six of Moran's men. Because 14 February is Valentine's Day, this became known as the Valentine's Day **Massacre**.

No one could prove that Capone was behind the killing. But a few years later he was caught for tax **fraud**. He was 32 and went to prison for 7 years. This ended his power at last.

STILL FAMOUS

Al Capone (below) was let out of prison in 1939, at the age of 40. Just 8 years later he died of a **stroke**. He was buried in Mount Olivet Cemetery, Chicago. Films of his life of crime have kept his name alive around the world. The first film based on his life was *Scarface* in 1932.

'BABY FACE' NELSON

'Baby Face' (above) was born in 1908, in Chicago. By the age of 14, he was a car thief. He was called 'Baby Face' because he looked so young. He became a bank robber and joined The Dillinger Gang in 1934. He shot many policemen and FBI agents but was eventually killed in a gun battle.

Chicago's Biograph Theatre where Dillinger was shot.

GANG LIFE AND DEATH

Many violent people joined **bootlegger** gangs in the 1920s. One was George 'Machine Gun' Kelly. His wife was also a bootlegger but she wanted more. She got George a machine gun and made him practise shooting. He joined a bank-robbing gang as their machine-gunner and held up many banks.

It was George's wife's idea to kidnap a millionaire called Charles Urschel. They demanded a **ransom** of $200,000. They almost got away with it, but the ransom money was traced back to them.

Kelly was sent to jail in Alcatraz Prison, the famous high-security prison built off the coast of San Francisco in the USA. He died there in 1954.

FBI Federal Bureau of Investigation, which deals with serious crime in the USA

DILLINGER

John Dillinger was a name everyone feared. He was a robber and a murderer. In the early 1930s, Dillinger and his violent gang robbed banks and police stations in the USA. He broke out of prison three times, killing guards as he did so. The Dillinger Gang killed yet another policeman in a Chicago bank robbery. The **FBI** set out to stop him once and for all.

One night in 1934, Dillinger took two friends to a cinema in Chicago. One of them had warned the FBI, so they were waiting for him. Five shots were fired and John Dillinger died in the street, aged just 31.

ORDINARY

Johnnie's just an ordinary fellow. Of course he goes out and holds up banks and things, but he's really just like any other fellow.

Mary Kinder, John Dillinger's girlfriend

GET · DILLINGER!
$15,000 Reward

A PROCLAMATION

WHEREAS, One John Dillinger stands charged officially with numerous felonies including murder in several states and his banditry and depredation stamp him as an outlaw, a fugitive from justice and a vicious menace to life and property;

NOW, THEREFORE, We, Paul McNutt, Governor of Indiana; George White, Governor of Ohio; F. B. Olson, Governor of Minnesota; William A. Comstock, Governor of Michigan; and Henry Horner, Governor of Illinois, do hereby proclaim and offer a reward of Five Thousand Dollars ($5,000.00) to be paid to the person or persons who apprehend and deliver the said John Dillinger into the custody of any sheriff of any of the above-mentioned states or his duly authorized agent.

THIS IS IN ADDITION TO THE $10,000.00 OFFERED BY THE FEDERAL GOVERNMENT FOR THE ARREST OF JOHN DILLINGER.

HERE IS HIS FINGERPRINT CLASSIFICATION and DESCRIPTION. ———— FILE THIS FOR IDENTIFICATION PURPOSES.

John Dillinger. (w) age 30 yrs., 5-8½. 170½ lbs., gray eyes, med. chest, hair, med. comp., med. build. Dayton, O., P. D. No. 10587. O. S. E. No. 559-646.

F.P.C. (12)
M 9 R O O
S 14 U OO 8
13 10 O O O
u R w w w
5 11 15 I S
u U u w u

FRONT VIEW

Be on the lookout for this desperado. He is heavily armed and usually is protected with bullet-proof vest. Take no unnecessary chances in getting this man. He is thoroughly prepared to shoot his way out of any situation.

GET HIM
DEAD
OR ALIVE

Notify any Sheriff or Chief of Police of Indiana, Ohio, Minnesota, Michigan, Illinois.

or THIS BUREAU

SIDE VIEW

ILLINOIS STATE BUREAU OF CRIMINAL IDENTIFICATION
T. P. Sullivan, Supt.

THE GANG

The Mafia is an organized **international** body of criminals that began in Sicily in Europe. It is now widespread around the world, especially in Italy and the USA.

Criminal gangs were at work in Italy and on the nearby island of Sicily for centuries. By the 19th century, some of these gangs had joined up to form an organization called the Mafia. Joining the Mafia gave members pride, power and protection. If anyone cheated them, they just asked a Mafia hit man to pay a visit. But no one would cheat on a member of his or her own gang, called a 'family'.

Mafia members spread through all Italian cities. Some were wanted for murder so many left Italy. They went to other countries where the Italian police could not arrest them. In the 1870s, many headed for the USA.

The birth place of the Mafia.

international   involves more than one country

THE US MAFIA

All big cities have their criminal gangs. The big cities of the USA in the 1900s were just right for gangs like these to **thrive**.

America was a new country that offered **immigrants** a new life. Most immigrants brought work, energy and ideas. But a few brought other ideas, about crime. These ideas attracted more criminal immigrants. They teamed up to organize **illegal** gambling, drinking and **racketeering**. In fact, they attracted the biggest network of criminals from Europe. Their name was already well known. The Mafia had arrived.

By the 1920s, the Mafia was running a network of organized criminal businesses in the USA. Its power began to spread across the whole country.

TODAY

Mafia gangs are still active in New York and New Orleans. In fact, Italian **organized crime** is big business around the world. Experts in Italy think this organized crime is worth over $100 billion each year. Although the Mafia does not have as much power as it used to, it may be behind a lot of this crime.

Mess with us and someone could get hurt ...it won't be us!

thrive   do very well

NEW YORK

New York's gangs included the Plug Uglies, the Dead Rabbits and the Five-Points Gang. They often got into fights. Irish and Italian gangs clashed all the time.

One of the most powerful Italian Mafia leaders was Nicholas Morello. In 1916, he went to make peace with his enemy, Pelligrino Morano. But Morano's men were waiting with machine guns. They shot Morello dead. Morano was shocked when the **bribes** he paid the New York Police did not keep him out of prison. For him, crime did not pay after all.

CRIME ON THE SCREEN

Many films about **organized crime** have been set in New York. *Gangs of New York* (below) is about two **rival** gangs in the 1860s. In the film, a gang called the Natives, led by 'the Butcher', is at war with the Dead Rabbits, an Irish **immigrant** gang.

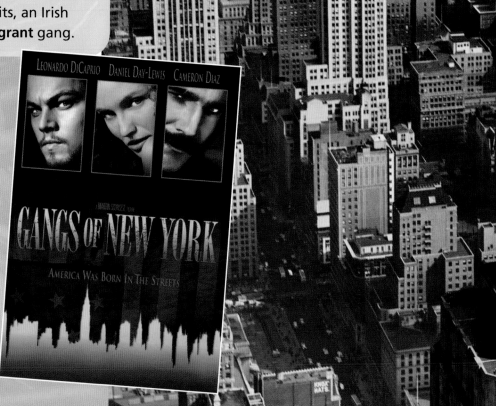

LEONARDO DICAPRIO   DANIEL DAY-LEWIS   CAMERON DIAZ

GANGS OF NEW YORK

AMERICA WAS BORN IN THE STREETS

contract   agreement, in this case an illegal agreement to kill a person for money

FAMILY MOBS

The next Mafia **godfather** to rule New York was Charlie Luciano. He joined other **mobsters** to make five families. They divided the city into five main Mafia gangs.

In 1929, Luciano was kidnapped and stabbed with an ice-pick. He survived but still kept *omerta*. This is a **vow** never to reveal Mafia secrets, including the names of the people who had stabbed him!

By 1935, Luciano was known as the Boss of Bosses. He ruled with force but ended up in prison. During World War 2, he gave the US Navy important information about Sicily. In return, the US Government let him return to Italy to live. Luciano died of a heart attack in 1962 while planning a film of his life story.

MURDER INC.

The Mafia needed to hire killers to get rid of their enemies. A gang called Murder Inc. made it their business to murder people. Throughout the 1930s, Murder Inc. did many **contract** killings for gangs in New York. It was responsible for 500 to 700 murders around the USA.

As more Mafia members moved into town, crime became big business in New York.

mobster   Mafia boss of one of the mobs
vow   promise

LATER DAYS

John Gotti was born in 1940 and left school at 16 to join the Gambino gang. This was one of the five Mafia families that controlled New York at the time. In the 1980s, Gotti became its boss.

Gotti dressed in smart suits and pretended to be a salesman. He was really a ruthless **mobster**. The **FBI** knew this but they did not have enough proof to put him behind bars. In 1992, Gotti was at last sent to prison for life, for six murders and **racketeering**. He died in prison in 2002.

NOT OVER

In the 1990s, the FBI said there were at least 25 Mafia gangs across the USA, with thousands of members. The FBI still deals with the effects of the Mafia today.

The FBI headquarters in Washington, USA.

Cosa Nostra criminal organization that grew out of Mafia gangs

RECENT TIMES

The 'five families' of New York brought terror to the city for 70 years. President Kennedy tried to control the Mafia's power in the 1960s. When he was **assassinated** in 1963, there were rumours that Mafia members were involved. These **rumours** have never been proven.

Police seize goods **smuggled** by organized gangs.

The Mafia's power in America today is nothing like it used to be. But it is still behind some drug and gun dealing, **fraud** and **money laundering**. Money laundering is a big criminal business. The Mafia helps criminals to disguise stolen cash as legal savings. This stops the police finding out where cheques and bank notes come from. Money laundering also **invests** the Mafia bosses' **profits** to make sure they cannot be traced so they 'stay clean'.

STILL FIGHTING

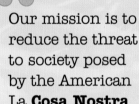

Our mission is to reduce the threat to society posed by the American La **Cosa Nostra** (LCN) and Italian Organized Crime (IOC). Our goal is to get rid of these criminal organizations in the United States. To do this, we work to reduce their power and membership.

FBI Organized Crime Section

John Gotti was known as the 'Dapper Don'.

money laundering   turning stolen money into legal savings or shares in businesses

CRIME AROUND THE WORLD

Criminal gangs are active all around the world.

CAN YOU BELIEVE IT?

Nearly a thousand small organized crime groups work in the UK. Most are British-born gangs, although Colombian, Italian, Chinese, Russian and Jamaican **gangsters** work in London, Manchester, Glasgow and Belfast. The biggest business for all these gangs is drug **smuggling**.

UK

The docks and warehouses in the East End of London made rich pickings for thieves in the 1950s and 1960s. As well as robbery, the gangs organized **protection rackets**. This meant people had to pay to avoid being attacked. Gang fights were common. Each gang tried to get more power than its **rival**.

The Kray brothers are one of the most famous British criminal families of the last 50 years. Reggie and Ronnie Kray were twins who started out as youth gang leaders in the 1950s. After **deserting** the British army, they became gangland bosses in London's tough East End.

East End docklands in the 1960s.

CRIME FACT
52 murders in the UK in 1999 were thought to be linked to organized crime.

WORD BANK deserting   running away from being in the army, which is illegal

MAFIA LINKS IN THE UK

The Krays were quick with their fists. Both were bullies who demanded payment to leave people alone. With their older brother, the Kray twins ruled pubs and gambling houses. No one upset 'The Firm', as they were called.

In the early 1960s 'The Firm' made contact with the US Mafia to set up business deals in London. Ronnie became very violent and ruled through fear. An ex-gang member upset him so the Krays killed him. In 1969, the twins were sentenced to 35 years in prison for this murder. The three Kray brothers are now dead and their family empire of **organized crime** is over.

FINAL CHAPTER

Reggie Kray was the last of the big-time London East End gangsters. His death in prison in 2000 finally ended their story. Ten years earlier, a film called *The Krays* earned him a lot of money. But he could not spend much of it from inside his prison cell!

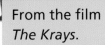

From the film *The Krays*.

RUSSIA

The Russian Mafiya has been organizing crime in Russia for years. It organizes **fraud, forgery**, and smuggling people. One group, called the Red Mafiya, deals in stolen art and antiques. Many Russian treasures have been **smuggled** abroad.

FISHY BUSINESS

Caviar smuggling is a crime that is **unique** to Russian gangs. Caviar is an expensive food made from the eggs of **sturgeon** fish. 75 per cent of the world's caviar comes from Russian sturgeon caught in the River Volga and the Caspian Sea. **Poaching** and smuggling by organized gangs has made sturgeon very rare.

DID YOU KNOW?

Over a hundred large criminal organizations are at work in Russia. Russia's Department for Fighting Organized Crime thinks there are another 5000 smaller criminal groups, which launder money and smuggle drugs.

Many of Russia's criminal gangs are based in the capital city of Moscow.

extinct   died out, never to return
forgery   making false documents, money or paintings

Once poachers pull a sturgeon on to their boat, they cut it open to scoop out its eggs. They pack them into cans and throw the dead fish back overboard. This 'Caviar Mafiya' has fast transport links to get their **illegal** caviar out of the country. By **bribing** police at **checkpoints**, they can get across borders and escape.

THE LAW

The legal caviar business is now at great risk because sturgeon fish are becoming **extinct**. The giant beluga is the largest and most highly prized type of sturgeon. It has almost disappeared. That means people will pay even more for illegal caviar. Sturgeon fishing is now against the law.

BIG MONEY
Russia's legal sales of sturgeon dropped from 10,000 tonnes in 1992 to 500 tonnes in 2002. In parts of Europe and the USA, a few tiny spoonfuls of Russian caviar (above) sell for over US $100. The world shortage puts the price up even higher. No wonder organized gangs make big money.

poaching   stealing animals by fishing or hunting illegally
unique   nothing else like it

ASIA

China, Japan, Hong Kong and Taiwan have their own criminal gangs similar to Mafia families. One of the names used for these is 'Tongs'. These go back hundreds of years. Today, much of their crime involves making, stealing and smuggling **heroin**.

Tongs also **smuggle** people. If anyone wants to get to another country to live, the Tongs can arrange it – for a fee. They organize a lot of **illegal immigration**, charging huge fees to smuggle families out of Asia to the USA. The people are often packed like sheep into boats. The Tongs do not care, as long as they get their money.

HONG KONG

The Sun Yee On is the name of a large criminal organization in Hong Kong (above). It has about 56,000 members. Its gangs control crime in the streets. One of their interests is expensive cars. Thousands of cars have gone missing from Hong Kong's streets. Stolen cars can be sold for good money.

Philadelphia's Chinatown.

WORD BANK   economy   anything to do with money and finances

SLAVE LABOUR

Once families get to the USA, they hope for a better life. But the Tongs still run their lives. Many illegal **immigrants** end up in **slave labour**. The Tongs are thought to run many clothes factories in Philadelphia, within a few kilometres of the city's Chinatown area.

Even if immigrants manage to set up their own businesses, Tong gangs will demand protection money. That means a weekly payment to the gang. Otherwise the Tongs burn down the business or attack the owner. The Tongs rule by fear.

BIG PROBLEM

The Chinese police believe there may be as many as 150,000 criminal gangs in Hong Kong and Taiwan (below). They are tied up with much of the business that goes on. This must cause a lot of harm to the **economy** in this part of Asia.

slave labour   being made to work hard for long hours with little pay

CHINA AND JAPAN

Many Chinese criminal gangs belong to an organization called the Triad. They work around the world, mainly in the Chinese districts of big cities. They run everything from drug and cigarette **smuggling** to gambling. But many of the gangs are best known for violence. Wars between Triad gangs have ended in murder.

PARTNERS IN CRIME

Tong gangs are secret Chinese groups involved in **organized crime**, such as people-smuggling. Many of these are based in the USA.

Today, Triads are Asian gangs that specialize in drug smuggling and armed robbery. The 14k Triad is the largest triad worldwide. It was formed after World War 2.

March, 2001

'Triad' schoolboys caught in Hong Kong

Eleven schoolboys have been arrested in Hong Kong. They were helping a triad crime gang to sell drugs and **pirate copies** of videos. Triads have been using boys as young as 12 or 13 years old in some of their businesses. Fourteen adults were also arrested in raids.

Actors protest against Triads in the Hong Kong film industry.

WORD BANK

disobey   break the rules or the law
offender   someone who breaks a rule or the law

YAKUZA

In 1992, Japan banned all Yakuza criminal gangs. These gangs go back almost 300 years. In the 1950s, there were over 5000 gangs across Japan. Today there are fewer.

Many Yakuza wear sunglasses, slicked down hair and some have fingers missing. Fingers are cut off if gang rules are broken! The first time a member **disobeys**, the top joint of the little finger is cut off. The freshly chopped finger-tip is wrapped in a cloth and handed to the **offender's** boss. Next time, the whole finger is chopped off. A bad member may soon have no fingers at all!

MEN ONLY

The Yakuza do not trust women. They believe that women cannot fight like men. If there is a fight, a member must be ready to fight to the death, rather than lose the battle. Yakuza members must be willing to die for their boss. Their leader is called an 'oyaban'.

Yakuza members cover their bodies with tattoos.

The samurai sword is ideal for a fight to the death – or for chopping fingers off!

pirate copy   CD, DVD or video that has been copied illegally

AUSTRALIA

In the early 1900s, many Mafia members left Italy. They settled not only in the USA, but also in Australia. Some learned how to make fast money. They went to **remote** farms and made threats of violence unless the farmers paid protection money.

DUNGEONS

The dungeons of the Court of Victoria in Australia were used from 1884 to the 1950s. They were opened to the public in 2003. Les 'Squizzy' Taylor was once locked up there. He was the Melbourne **organized crime** boss of the 1920s. He ran a gang until he was killed in a gunfight in 1927.

cannabis   dried leaves of the hemp plant; smoked or chewed as a drug

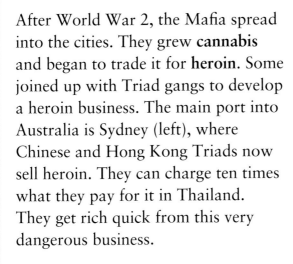

After World War 2, the Mafia spread into the cities. They grew **cannabis** and began to trade it for **heroin**. Some joined up with Triad gangs to develop a heroin business. The main port into Australia is Sydney (left), where Chinese and Hong Kong Triads now sell heroin. They can charge ten times what they pay for it in Thailand. They get rich quick from this very dangerous business.

Recent newspapers have told of the drugs threat from organized criminals.

GANGS INVADE AUSTRALIA

Eastern European gangs are a frightening new force in Australia's **underworld**. The ruthless **gangsters** are behind Melbourne's heroin trade. Some have links to the Russian Mafiya. To make bigger **profits**, the gangs add powder to the heroin to make it go further. This means the drugs they sell on the street can be **lethal**.

Russian gangs came to Australia in the 1990s. Some organize theft. Others **forge** passports for **illegal immigrants**. They tend to be violent, too. When these criminals say 'I'm going to kill you', they mean it.

NEW ZEALAND

Triads and other organized criminal gangs have also settled in New Zealand. Some of the 14K Triad and the San Yee On arrived in the 1970s. Most major heroin raids in New Zealand have involved these criminal gangs. Attacks on the police are rare in New Zealand. This may change if organized crime keeps growing.

BIG BUSINESS

WORD BANK cartel organized group that controls the making and selling of a product

Thousands of people around the world are part of the **illegal** drugs business. They might grow the plants, make the drugs, **smuggle** them or buy and sell them. They are all part of this massive **organized crime**. The business makes the bosses very rich. It makes other people very poor and very ill.

Columbia in South America is one of the well-known areas for growing and making cocaine. This drug is made from the cocoa plant. Groups of people who make the drugs and sell them are called **cartels**. Colombian drug cartels are large organized gangs. They provide 80 per cent of the world's cocaine.

A HUGE PROBLEM

The **United Nations** reports that there are more than 50 million regular users of heroin, cocaine and other drugs around the world. The trade in illegal drugs could be worth as much as US $400 billion a year. Organized gangs are behind most of the drug production.

Police seize cocaine in Peru.

DRUG SMUGGLING

The bosses of the drug gangs are often called drug **barons**. They find all sorts of ways to smuggle drugs into different countries. The US police once learned that a Colombian drug cartel planned to buy a submarine. What better way to avoid getting caught than to smuggle drugs under water?

Other drug smugglers use animals. When crates of snakes have been searched on ships, strange things have been found. Balloons filled with **heroin** have been found inside boa constrictors! Smugglers once hid heroin in the cages of deadly snakes. The security guards were meant to be scared off from searching the cage. The plan did not work.

HEROIN

Heroin is made from the opium poppy (below). But this multi-million dollar business does not use the latest high-speed transport. Much of Europe's heroin starts off on camels! These animals carry the drugs through Afghanistan into Eastern Europe. The heroin is then smuggled on into markets in the UK, Holland and Germany.

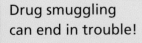
Drug smuggling can end in trouble!

PEOPLE-SMUGGLING

Human **migration** is nothing new. For centuries, people have left their homes to find a better life in another country. Today more and more people from poor countries try to move to Western Europe, Australia and North America. Criminal gangs are always there to help – for money.

The criminals promise to take **migrants** to a better life. But they do not tell them the full story. Often the migrants are squashed into small trucks or boats. **Hygiene** on the boats is poor. What little food and water they have soon runs out. The journey can be total misery, or even **fatal**.

Illegal immigrants were squashed to death in this truck.

endangered species   animals in danger of becoming extinct

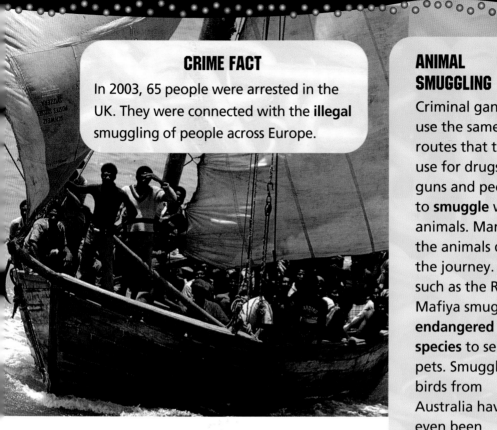

CRIME FACT

In 2003, 65 people were arrested in the UK. They were connected with the **illegal** smuggling of people across Europe.

ANIMAL SMUGGLING

Criminal gangs use the same routes that they use for drugs, guns and people to **smuggle** wild animals. Many of the animals die on the journey. Gangs such as the Russian Mafiya smuggle **endangered species** to sell as pets. Smuggled birds from Australia have even been swapped for **heroin** in Thailand.

TERROR

The crew and guards on the boats can be violent. Sick people are often thrown overboard.
In stormy seas, the crowded boats are at great risk.

Getting to shore can be dangerous, too. It may mean steering the boat along a rocky coast in the dark. The migrants have to scramble or swim to shore without getting caught by the police. Because they are now **illegal immigrants**, they must obey the gang who brought them in. This often means working for the gang for many years to pay off the huge cost of the journey. If not, their family back home must pay up or face torture. Or even death.

migration   travelling long distances to find a new home
migrant   someone who travels to a new country to live

MISSING ART – REWARD €530,000

An oil painting by the famous painter Pablo Picasso was stolen from a yacht in 1999. The ship *Coral Island* was docked in the French port of Antibes. An organized gang of thieves stole a work of art called *Dora Maar*, (above) which is worth £4 million. So far, there is no news of the painting.

ART SMUGGLING

Many paintings, pieces of pottery and jewellery are worth a fortune. But if thieves try to break into a house, a museum or a gallery to steal one of the treasures, they have a problem. They must sell the art to get their money. They will get caught when dealers know the work is stolen.

Organized crime gangs work with a network of criminal dealers. They will **smuggle** the art out of the country quickly. They might demand **ransom** money for the art to be returned. Or they may find a buyer who does not mind if the art is stolen. Either way, art theft can make organized criminals rich.

These stolen antiques were found by French police.

corrupt   dishonest or damaged through bribery and fraud

Nine paintings from the art collection of Russia's famous living artist, Sergei Bugayev, have been stolen. They disappeared from Bugayev's home outside St Petersburg. The missing works are valued at US $250,000. When Bugayev discovered the theft, he called the local police. When they arrived, the police refused to take any action. They said there was no **evidence** of a break-in.

So why didn't the police believe Bugayev? Many people think that the Russian Mafiya **bribe** the police to ignore their crimes. Organized crime **thrives** if the local police are **corrupt**. Once the criminals pay the police, they can even get away with murder.

Police at Drumlanrig Castle investigate the missing painting *Madonna with Yarnwinder*.

MISSING ART – REWARD £1 MILLION

In 2003, thieves stole a painting from Drumlanrig Castle in Scotland (below). The picture was by the famous artist Leonardo da Vinci. It was called *Madonna with Yarnwinder*.

The police found the getaway car abandoned not far from the castle. But the theft is still a mystery. The painting is worth up to £30 million. Where is it?

evidence   proof or information from the scene of a crime

FIGHTING BACK

The misery, terror and cost from crime gangs affect all countries. Air travel and the **Internet** have made **organized crime** a **global** problem of the 21st century. It is very easy to do deals and travel all over the world. Small gangs of bullies can now join a huge network. But the police forces around the world can also join up. When criminals travel from country to country, an **international** police force is watching. It is called **Interpol**.

Interpol was set up for tracking down organized crime that operates around the world. Today, it is the biggest police organization. There are 181 member countries over five continents. Interpol never sleeps!

Interpol   international police force that works across many countries

INTERPOL

Interpol allows police forces to work together. They can quickly share information about criminal gangs on the move. Much of its work involves finding out about gangs and tracking where they are. Their crimes are usually to do with **trafficking** of weapons, drugs and human beings. The other big crimes are **money laundering**, **cyber crime** and terrorism.

Interpol works around the clock. It receives, stores and sends information to all its member countries. Sometimes this will be in the form of 'wanted' posters. Details of criminals and their gangs can flash around the world in seconds. Now there is no corner where criminals can hide from the law.

Have you seen this person?

PFAHLS, LUDWIG HOLGER
Born: 13/12/1942
Nationality: German
Age today:
61 years old

The German authorities are offering a reward of €5,000 for information that leads to the capture of Dr PFAHLS.

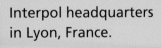

Interpol headquarters in Lyon, France.

FACT OR FICTION?

A lot of stories are told about the Mafia. People imagine men in long coats, hats and dark glasses waiting in the shadows. Under their arms they carry a violin case. The case holds a machine gun. This is just one of the **myths** about how Mafia members look.

DO NOT BELIEVE IT!

Wild stories warn you to beware in Moscow. They say the Russian Mafiya watch every street, ready to kidnap any visitor. Tyres squeal as a black car with blackened windows whisks away yet another victim. Kidnaps do happen, but most tourists are safe.

James Cagney in the 1938 film *Angels with Dirty Faces*.

myth   made-up tale, told over the years and handed on

Marlon Brando in *The Godfather* (1972), another film about the mafia.

FAR-FETCHED

Films often give a false image of a typical Mafia boss. In real life they are unlikely to say the words they speak in films.

" I'm gonna make you an offer you can't refuse. Two of us can keep a secret... as long as one of us is dead... "

THE WRONG IDEA

From the world of James Bond to television series like *The Sopranos*, **organized crime** makes good entertainment. Old **gangster** films of the 1940s also gave audiences false ideas about criminal gangs. Books, films and television help to keep many of the myths going. They can also make criminals seem exciting. Or they can give the wrong idea that all **immigrants** from Italy, Russia or China belong to dangerous gangs.

Another myth is that the Mafia makes big money from sport. They place their bets then fix the events. A few threats to a referee or goalkeeper then makes sure a particular team wins. Simple – but false!

IN THE NEWS

Newspapers report **organized crime** all the time. Some of the biggest stories happen when gang leaders go to prison.

Hard Times For The Mafia

New York, 2003

New York's five Mafia family bosses are all behind bars for the first time.

Joseph Massino was the last to be jailed. He was said to be the boss of the Bonanno crime family.

Peter Gotti was the head of the Gambino crime family. Now he is in prison, too. He follows a family **tradition** of getting locked up. Since the 1990s, the Gambino gang has appeared in more books and television programmes than any other Mafia family.

THE JAILING OF JOSEPH MASSINO

" There was a time when no mob boss was even **convicted**. This is one more step in the fight against the mob. **"**

Ronald Goldstock, former head of the New York Organized Crime Task Force, 2003

Peter Gotti was the brother of mobster John Gotti (on the right).

WORD BANK   convicted   found guilty and punished

BACK IN THE NEWS

Roberto Calvi was the head of an Italian bank. He also had links with members of the Mafia in Sicily. In 1982, he lost the bank a lot of money. He went on the run to London, using a false passport. Two days later he was found dead, hanging from Blackfriars Bridge. It was a mystery. The police thought he must have killed himself because of all his worries. His family said it must have been murder. In 2003, twenty-one years later, more **evidence** came to light. Tests suggested that Roberto Calvi was murdered by the Mafia. Maybe they wanted to stop him telling their secrets.

MAFIA LINK?

A study into Roberto Calvi's death took 4 years. It showed that he was killed in a builders' yard. His killers then took his body by boat to Blackfriars Bridge (below), where they hanged him. In 2003 Calvi's son said a trial would one day convict his father's killers.

tradition   custom or event that happens down the years

TIMES CHANGE

The Mafia is the biggest single **shareholder** in the American **economy**... They have more influence on the daily lives of all Americans than the government or Wall Street or even the Church. They can **manipulate** anything.

Joe Coffey, Commander in Chief of Detectives Organized Crime Homicide Task Force, New York Police Department, 1978

Organized crime is here to stay. Ever since the first gang met to organize a hold-up, the world has had to deal with criminals working together. Their methods have become more **professional**, with no thought for the people they harm. So how will organized crime change in the next 10 years?

Smuggling of people, drugs and weapons will always happen. But other organized criminals are likely to become threats to the security of countries. If gangs get hold of nuclear or chemical weapons, they may be able to make all sorts of demands. Perhaps it is just a matter of time.

Police help make the world a far safer place than it could be.

WORD BANK

majority   greater part
manipulate   deal with something to your own advantage

KEEPING ONE STEP AHEAD

By 2015, experts think criminal groups will be far more involved in **cyber crime**. They could **disrupt** government, police and bank computers. **Interpol** is already keeping a close eye on this.

Criminals might get bigger, bolder and more organized. But so will Interpol. Police and governments will continue to protect the **majority** of people. It is the majority, after all, who are honest, keeping the world far safer.

NEW TIMES, OLD PROBLEMS...

Crime changes and adapts to different times. Professional gangs will always try to get rich at the expense of others. Some people argue that banning drink, drugs and gambling will make the world safer. Others say that this will just let criminals run more **illegal** businesses and make huge **profits**. There will never be easy answers in the fight to stop organized crime.

Banning alcohol in the 1920s led to even more crime.

THE FORTY THIEVES

Madame St Clair, known as Queenie, ran a gang in New York in the 1920s. She called it The Forty Thieves. The gang was so tough that all the other **mobsters** left her and her turf well alone!

If you want to find out more about the criminal underworld, why not have a look at these books:

Behind the Scenes: Solving a Crime, Peter Mellet (Heinemann Library, 1999)

Forensic Files: Investigating Murders, Paul Dowswell (Heinemann Library, 2004)

Forensic Files: Investigating Thefts and Heists, Alex Woolf (Heinemann Library, 2004)

Just the Facts: Cyber Crime, Neil McIntosh (Heinemann Library, 2002)

DID YOU KNOW?

In Australia it is a crime in some states to:

- own a mattress without a mattress licence
- wear pink hot pants after midday on Sundays
- change a light bulb unless you are an electrician!

CRIMINAL RECORDS

- The world's first speeding ticket was issued in the UK in 1896 to a man called Walter Arnold. He was travelling at 8 mph in a 2 mph zone.

- The most successful sniffer dog was a Labrador from the USA called Snag. He found 118 different hoards of hidden drugs worth an amazing £580 million!

- The oldest person to be hanged was 82 year old Allan Mair in 1843. He was hanged in the UK sitting down because he was unable to stand.

- The world's largest safe-deposit-box robbery took place in 1976. A group of highly-trained criminals stole more than £22 million worth of goods from a bank in the Middle East.

COSA NOSTRA

The name **Cosa Nostra**, or Mafia, means 'our thing'. It started hundreds of years ago in Sicily to protect ordinary local people from the police and from **bandits**.

GLOSSARY

assassinate to kill a leader

bandit robber or murderer member of a gang

baron powerful business person

blackmail threats to make someone pay

bootlegging smuggling illegal alcohol

bribing paying someone with influence to act illegally in your favour

cannabis dried leaves of the hemp plant; smoked or chewed as a drug

cartel organized group that controls the making and selling of a product

caviar expensive food made from the eggs of sturgeon fish

checkpoint border where guards inspect papers, vehicles etc.

contract agreement, in this case an illegal agreement to kill a person for money

convicted found guilty and punished

corrupt dishonest or damaged through bribery and fraud

Cosa Nostra crime organization that grew out of Mafia gangs

cyber crime crime involving computers and the Internet

deserting running away from being in the army, which is illegal

disobey break the rules or the law

disrupt interrupt or break up

economy anything to do with money and finances

endangered species animals in danger of becoming extinct

evidence proof or information from the scene of a crime

executed killed as a punishment

extinct died out, never to return

fatal end in death

FBI Federal Bureau of Investigation, which deals with serious crime in the USA

fiction made-up story from the imagination

forgery making false documents, money or paintings

fraud false or dishonest trick to get money

gangster member of a criminal gang

global around the whole world

godfather name for the head of a Mafia 'family'

heroin highly addictive drug made from the opium poppy

hygiene standards of health and cleanliness

illegal against the law

illegal immigration arriving in another country without permission

immigrant settler in a new country from another part of the world

international involves more than one country

Internet worldwide network that links all computer networks together

Interpol international police force that works across many countries

invest put money into shares, business schemes or savings accounts

lethal dangerous and deadly

loyalty never letting anyone down and showing commitment

majority greater part

manipulate deal with something to your own advantage

massacre killing of lots of people

migrant someone who travels to a new country to live

migration travelling long distances to find a new home

mobster Mafia boss of one of the mobs

money laundering turning stolen money into legal savings or shares in businesses

myth made-up tale, told over the years and handed on

offender someone who breaks a rule or the law

organized crime large organizations involved in crimes in many countries

pirate copy CD, DVD or video that has been copied illegally

poaching stealing animals by fishing or hunting illegally

professional showing commitment and skill in a full-time occupation

profits money made by selling something higher than the price paid for it

prohibition when something is forbidden – such as making and selling alcohol

protection racket demanding money to 'protect' someone from being hurt by criminals

racketeering running a dishonest and illegal business

ransom payment demanded for the release of a prisoner

recruit new member

remote far away from towns and cities

rival person or team competing against one another

rumour story based on gossip

shareholder owns part of a company

slave labour being made to work hard for long hours with little pay

smuggle secretly bringing goods or people into or out of a country

stroke sudden illness caused by a clot of blood in the brain

sturgeon large shark-like fish, prized for its tiny eggs eaten as caviar by the rich

thrive do very well

tradition custom or event that happens down the years

trafficking movement between countries

underworld part of society that lives by organized crime

unique nothing else like it

United Nations world organization of countries formed in 1945 to promote peace and security

vow promise

INDEX